I WANT TO TELL YOU

I Want to Tell You

Cover Background 'Null' © Ryan Bliss (used with permission)
Back cover: The Hubble Deep Field. Credit: NASA/ESA
ISBN: 9798645034900
Independently Published

To my nephew Alex and his generation:

May you figure out what's going on,

and what part you want to have in it.

Foreword

When Julia sent me the other books in her "Bedtime Stories for Adults" series, I was delighted by their whimsical and simple profundity. They reminded me of something similar that I had written some years ago. By strange coincidence it was the topic of our conversation when we first met, in a little cafe in Paros, Greece, where she lived and I was a tourist. It was 2014, in April before the hordes of tourists descended and overwhelmed the place, so the shops and restaurants were glad to see us, and we drank strong red wine and found that we were both philosophers. Julia looked me in the eyes, as if searching to see if I really was 'there', I looked into hers. A bond was created that still nourishes us today despite living on opposite sides of the planet.

Julia shared with me some of her insights from Jungian psychology, taking delight in flight through the invisible realms. I offered that the fundamental error of humans everywhere is that we confuse the map with the territory and make our ideas more real than what the ideas refer to. It's easy to blame Plato for this - and I do - for his Theory of Forms in which ideas, and not the material world, possess the highest and most fundamental kind of reality. From that influence, Christianity, which is essentially a merging of Greek philosophy and Jewish mysticism, turned away from the divine feminine and the sacredness of this world, and turned its exclusive attention to God the Father, who art in heaven (and not on earth). But maybe that's another story.

A few months after meeting Julia, my brother Jerry asked me to contribute some spoken word to a project that my family was doing – making an album of Beatles' music. My family is full of talented musicians and singers and the songs of the Beatles have been an enduring common interest across the generations. So my brother brought aunts and nephews and nieces and siblings together into the professional recording studio of my nephew Rob and cut 16 songs of the Beatles, played, sung, and produced entirely by family and friends and put together the Family Beatles Album.

Many of the songs were not just covers, but reinterpretations. One of the songs was 'Tomorrow Never Knows', one of John Lennon's attempts at describing what happens during a psychedelic trip, based partly on his reading of the book *The Psychedelic Experience: A Manual Based on the Tibetan Book of the Dead* by Timothy Leary, Richard Alpert and Ralph Metzner. That song was on the Revolver album, released in 1966. The beginning lyrics are:

> *Turn off your mind, relax and float downstream, it is not dying.*
> *Lay down all thoughts, surrender to the void – it is shining.*
> *That you may see the meaning of within – it is being.*

In 1966 I was a 12 year-old Catholic schoolboy in suburban Los Angeles, where the revolution of the 60's had not yet reached and where I was still imagining I would grow up to be a "scientist/priest". But within a few years, like many other teenagers all over the world, my brother Jim and I along with our friends were obsessively listening to the Beatles' corpus to try to figure out what was going on, and what part we wanted to have in it.

Which is to say that when Jerry asked me to do spoken word on top of his reinterpretation of 'Tomorrow Never Knows', I didn't need to reread the lyrics to remind myself what the song was about. Still, I didn't know what I wanted to say, and it took me some months to send my contribution in. I knew what Jerry really wanted was for me to channel 'Gentle John', which is his slightly sardonic name for my priest/shaman persona that emerges now and again. So I put on my beginner's mind, found my innocent voice and all in one sitting wrote down the words that appear now in this book. I recorded it and sent it off to him. The feeling I have is that it came out of me from somewhere deeper than myself.

Jerry's version of the song is brilliant I think, with a tribal drum beat that adds a lot to the original. I feel my voice-over also recreates some of the earnestness and innocence of 1966 and the original song. All of which I credit to Jerry's vision of the song and to the others who played on and produced the album, who took those disparate elements and made them more than the sum of their parts. Here's the song: https://youtu.be/TtOdTILdFcg or google "youtube caron tomorrow never knows".

That same earnestness and innocence permeates Julia's self-published "Bedtime Stories for Adults". She and I have continued our philosophical conversations over these many years. I have so enjoyed creating this book with her, it is a perfect collaboration between us and a perfect summary of some of those conversations. As I told Julia that night in Paros, I'm a one beat drummer, and this is my one beat.

Love

John

I WANT TO
TELL YOU

Your mind experiences the world

and creates an internal
representation of it

and stores it inside of you.

This internal model is constructed from:

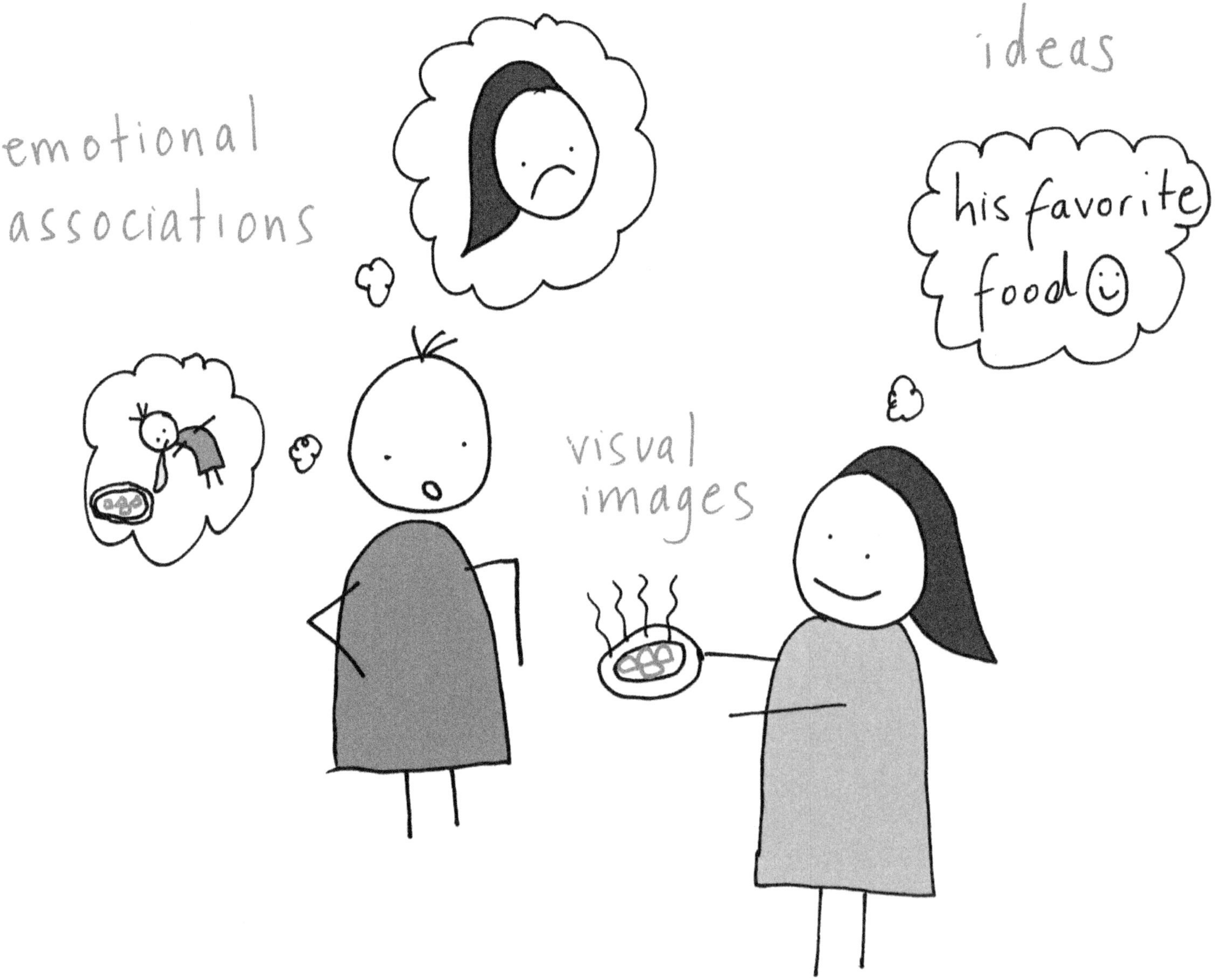

... and above all from

LANGUAGE

It's unbelievably useful, beautiful intricate machinery which mediates between the world and our experience of it.

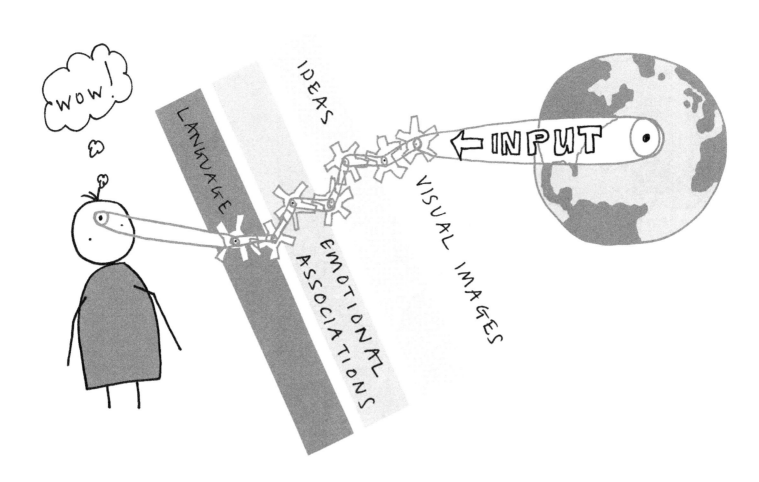

The problem is when we confuse the model of the world with the world itself.

We confuse the map
with the territory

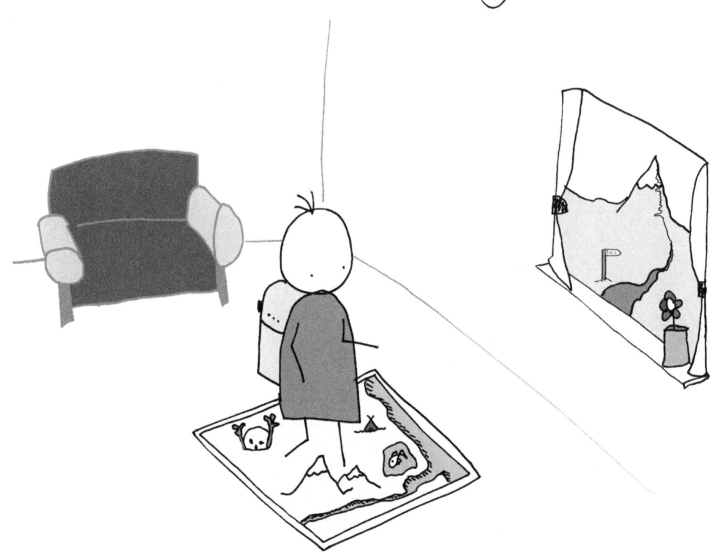

we believe what we think

...but what we think, comes from this mental representation; what we think **IS** this mental representation

what we experience becomes the words
that describe what we experience.

You can't think yourself
out of this box

You have to somehow free yourself from

Stop creating mental images that seem more real than the things they are images of.

The most important
image is the one
about our SELF

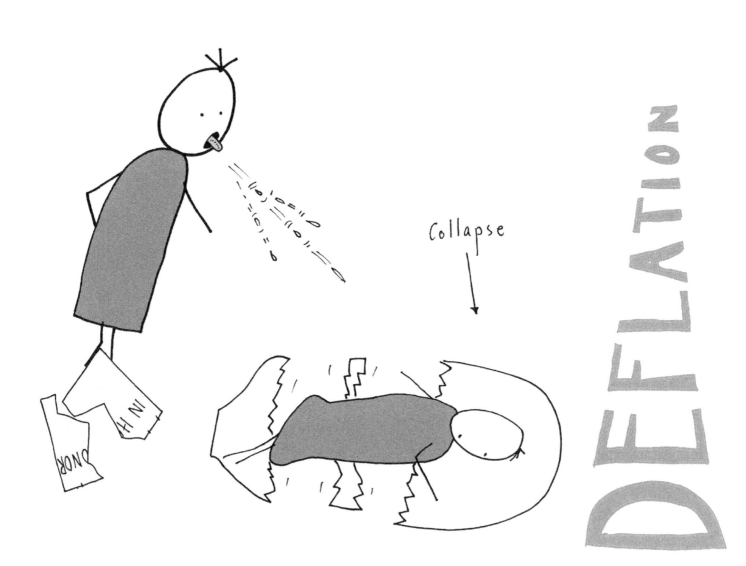

We mistake what we think about our self with who we actually are.

We identify with our thoughts,
& we think we are those thoughts.

Suppose there was a way to stop doing that? ...to become silent inside?

At first the mind does everything it can

to **DISTRACT YOU**

But eventually you come to the emptiness at the center of your self.

Most people run away as fast as they can at this point.

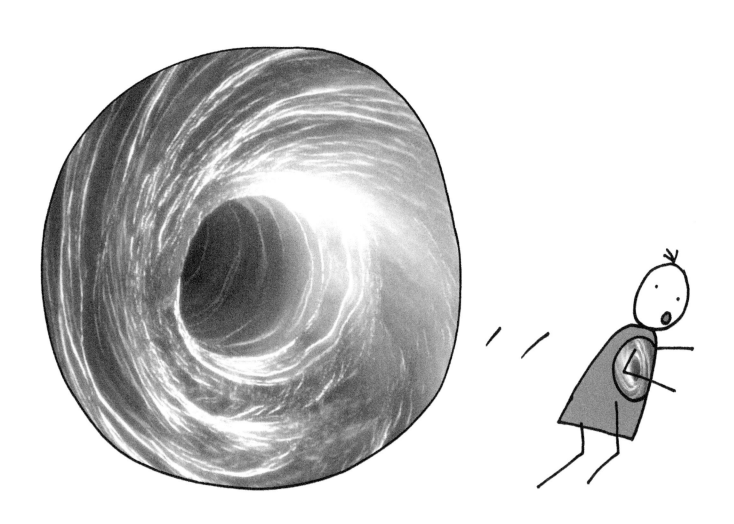

This is the

NOTHINGNESS

which contains

EVERYTHING

This is the Source.

This is God.

And It's inside of you.

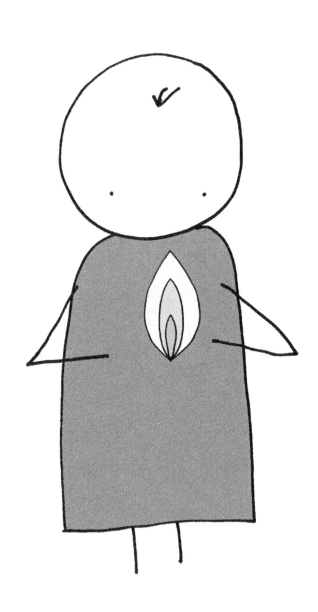

And it connects you to everything.

At the age of 15, John found that everything he believed was not true: god, church, america, father. Most of all, himself. That plunged him into his spiritual journey, and also into an undiagnosed depression. So he left home as soon as he could, fell in love and got his heart broken, found his tribe, studied physics and mathematics and philosophy, took psychedelics, worked hard as the working class must, grew up, became who he wanted to be, studied ballet and other dance for 7 years, fell in love and got his heart broken, started a software company, had children, worked hard to support them, grew up some more, moved to Colorado, studied computer science, got a divorce, revisited his depression this time with help from friends and therapists, found Contact Improvisation dance again, worked hard and took more psychedelics, became a big fish in a small pond like his father, did lots of other things, loved many people, became a grandfather, worked even harder, retired and wrote this book, and plans on writing more. Or not.

Julia Robinson has spent her life out of the box, hitchhiking around the world, floating down the Amazon in a self-made raft, selling roasted chickens in Argentina, working at an orphanage in Nepal, studying a masters in Jungian psychology in Catalonia, going to art school in Greece, dancing and writing in the States and living in nature in England. She is presently loving making music and writing in Latvia.

She has a curious mind, an adventurous spirit and ants in her pants. She travels much more now to realms within, guided by the *The Course in Miracles.*

She has written five books, prose, poetry and graphic existential meanders. She is a psychologist and facilitates on-line and presential *Therapy of Writing* explorations which are often nothing short of magical.

For more word whirlation, poems and information please visit:

w w w . i n t e n s e l y p e r s o n a l . c o m

BEDTIME STORIES FOR ADULTS

love

John & Julia

ppp

Thanks for reading !!..

More books by Julia Robinson

Bedtime Stories for Adults

Poetry

Poetry

Prose

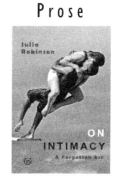

For more information please visit www.intenselypersonal.com

or search for any of these books/ebooks on Amazon

Printed in Great Britain
by Amazon